FOGGY AUTUMN MORNING
In the Creasey Mahan Nature Preserve

ALSO EXPLORE THESE BOOKS IN THE CREASEY MAHAN COLLECTION

One Foggy Morning in Winter
One Foggy Spring Morning
Spring
Summer
Foggy Summer Morning

FOGGY AUTUMN MORNING
In the Creasey Mahan Nature Preserve

Photography by Karin Acree

Copyright © 2019 by Karin Acree
All rights reserved.

Photographs taken by Karin Acree

Scripture quotations taken from the ESV® Bible (The Holy Bible, English Standard Version®), copyright © 2001 by Crossway, a publishing ministry of Good News Publishers. Used by permission. All rights reserved.

Scripture taken from The Message (MSG) copyright © 1993, 1994, 1995, 1996, 2000, 2001, 2002 by Eugene H. Peterson. Used by permission of NavPress Publishing Group.

Scripture quotations taken from the New American Standard Bible ® (NASB) Copyright © 1960, 1962, 1963, 1968, 1971, 1972, 1973, 1975, 1977, 1995 by The Lockman Foundation. Used by permission. www.Lockman.org.

Scripture quotations marked NIV are taken from The *Holy Bible*, N*ew International Version*® , NIV ® Copyright © 1973, 1978, 1984, 2011 by Biblica, Inc.™ Used by permission of Zondervan.

Scripture taken from the New King James Version®. Copyright © 1982 by Thomas Nelson. Used by permission. All rights reserved.

Scripture quotations marked NLT are taken from the *Holy Bible*, New Living Translation, copyright© 1996, 2004, 2015 by Tyndale House Foundation. Used by permission of Tyndale House Publishers, Inc., Carol Stream, Illinois 60188. All rights reserved.

This book or any portion thereof
may not be reproduced or used in an manner whatsoever
without the express written permission of the publisher
except for the use of brief quotations in a book review:

Printed in
The United States of America

ISBN: 9781937979485

Goshen, KY 40026
www.derekpublications.com

DEDICATION

*To our nation's
victims of
gun violence*

SHALOM

FORWARD
About the Creasey Mahan Collection

Karin's books represent well the words of poet and philosopher, Henry David Thoreau: "Heaven is under our feet as well as over our heads." Each photograph in this series captures a cherished moment – raindrops that look like jewels, a lightning bug as it rests on a leaf, sunlight streaming through trees and a Red-tailed Hawk soaring overhead. Her images are like prayers that remind us to slow down, enjoy each moment and behold every blessing that may appear before us.

When Karin first showed me her photographs and the accompanying passages contained in this series of scripture books, I was in awe of her talent, dedication and the many hours she spent alone and with her daughters, as they walked the scenic trails at Creasey Mahan Nature Preserve. The quotes that accompany the photographs match each image perfectly.

My hope is that you, the reader, will take time to let each image and scripture wash over you. Karin's books invite us to walk alongside her as she notices that "He has made everything beautiful in its time." (Ecclesiastes 3:11)

continued...

Creasey Mahan Nature Preserve is a public charity that serves nearly 50,000 visitors each year. Visitors may enjoy 170-acres of rolling hills, open grasslands, year-round streams, nine-miles of trails and a two-acre woodland garden. Families appreciate the annual events, Thrive Forest School programs, Forest Friends Playground and the Nature Center. Creasey Mahan is open 365 days a year from dawn to dusk.

By Tavia Cathcart Brown
Executive Director of Creasey Mahan Nature Preserve

Even though I walk through the valley of the shadow of death,
I fear no evil, for You are with me;
Your rod and Your staff, they comfort me.
PSALM 23:4 (NASB)

*The Light shines in the darkness,
and the darkness has not overcome it.*
JOHN 1:5 (ESV)

*You, LORD, are my lamp;
the LORD turns my darkness into light.*
2 SAMUEL 22:29 (NIV)

I called on your name, LORD, from the depths of the pit.
You heard my plea: "Do not close your ears to my cry for relief."
You came near when I called you, and you said, "Do not fear."
LAMENTATIONS 3:55-57 (NIV)

It is He who reveals the profound and hidden things;
He knows what is in the darkness,
And the light dwells with Him.
DANIEL 2:22 (ESV)

For there will be peace for the seed: the vine will yield its fruit, the land will yield its produce

and the heavens will give their dew - ZECHARIAH 8:12 (NASB)

But the path of the just is like the shining sun,

That shines ever brighter unto the perfect day. - PROVERBS 4:18 (NKJV)

Then Jesus said,
"Come to me, all of you who are weary and carry heavy burdens,
and I will give you rest.
MATTHEW 11:28 (NLT)

But for you who fear My name, the sun of righteousness will rise with healing in its wings
MALACHI 4:2 (NASB)

Jesus said to her, "I am the resurrection and the life. The one who believes in me will live, even though they die; and whoever lives by believing in me will never die. Do you believe this?"
JOHN 11:25-26 (NIV)

The LORD examines both the righteous and the wicked.
He hates those who love violence.
PSALM 11:5 (NLT)

May God our Father and Lord Jesus Christ
give you grace and peace.

God Offers Comfort to All

All praise to God,
the Father of our Lord Jesus Christ.
God is our merciful Father
and the source of all comfort.
He comforts us in all our troubles
so that we can comfort others.
When they are troubled,
we will be able to give them
the same comfort God has given us.
2 CORINTHIANS 1:2-4 (NLT)

God is our refuge and strength,
A very present help in trouble.
PSALM 46:1 (NKJV)

*Do not repay evil with evil or insult with insult.
On the contrary, repay evil with blessing,
because to this you were called so that you may inherit a blessing.
1 PETER 3:9 (NIV)*

But the fruit of the Spirit is love, joy, peace, forbearance,
kindness, goodness, faithfulness, gentleness and self control.
Against such things there is no law.
GALATIANS 5:22-23 (NIV)

Then your light will break forth
like the dawn,
and your healing will quickly appear;
then your righteousness will go before you,
and the glory of the LORD will be your
rear guard.
ISAIAH 58:8 (NIV)

Trust in the LORD with all your heart,
and do not lean on your own understanding.
In all your ways acknowledge him,
and he will make straight your paths.
PROVERBS 3:5-6 (ESV)

Be strong and courageous. Do not be afraid or terrified because of them, for the LORD your God goes with you; he will never leave you nor forsake you.
DEUTERONOMY 31:6 (NIV)

But LORD, be merciful to us,
for we have waited for you.
Be our strong arm each day
and our salvation in times of trouble.
ISAIAH 33:2 (NLT)

Blessed are those who mourn,
For they shall be comforted.
MATTHEW 5:4 (NKJV)

Don't worry about anything; instead, pray about everything.
Tell God what you need, and thank him for all he has done.
PHILIPPIANS 4:6 (NLT)

I will not leave you as orphans:
I will come to you.
JOHN 14:18 (NKJV)

God has said,
"I will never leave you;
never will I forsake you."
HEBREWS 13:5 (NIV)

*Remain in me, and I will remain in you.
For a branch cannot produce fruit if it is severed from the vine,
and you cannot be fruitful unless you remain in me.
JOHN 15:4 (NLT)*

But let justice roll down like waters
and righteousness like an
ever-flowing stream.
AMOS 5:24 (ESV)

*For if you forgive others their trespasses,
your heavenly Father will also forgive you,
but if you do not forgive others their trespasses,
neither will your Father forgive your trespasses.*
MATTHEW 6:14-15 (ESV)

I pray that God, the source of hope, will fill you completely with joy and peace because you trust in him.
Then you will overflow with confident hope through the power of the Holy Spirit.
ROMANS 15:13 (NLV)

Peace I leave with you, My peace I give to you;
not as the world gives do I give to you.
Let not your heart be troubled, neither let it be afraid.
JOHN 14:27 (NKJV)

SHALOM

ABOUT THE ACREE'S

Karin is a hard-working wife and mother of two lovely teenage daughters. Daily work and family demands are juggled with agile imperfection. To remain centered, and as time permits, she likes to cook, work out at the Y, play piano, paint (her husband Tony claims she's addicted), read, and to commune with nature--and with God--hiking through the woods.

ACKNOWLEDGEMENTS

I mindfully and prayerfully compiled this scripture photo book of numerous treks through the Creasey Mahan Nature Preserve with the guidance of many family and friends. I would like to extend my thanks to Bill Noel who sat down with me to improve my photography skills. If you see a difference in this book vs. the others, you can thank Bill! My thanks, also, to Tavia Brown and the wonderful staff at Creasey Mahan Nature Preserve.

DEDICATION
To our nation's victims of gun violence

I began taking these photographs in early autumn with a heavy heart. I was busy at work one morning in late September when my sister called. We typically don't talk during the day, so I knew something was wrong. "Everyone's OK," she said. And then she explained there had been a workplace shooting where our niece and nephew are employed in Middleton, WI. *No, no, no, no, NO!* A voice yelled in my head. *How could this happen?* I didn't feel numb....I was angry...I was FURIOUS that another redundant mass shooting had occurred in our country and like so many other victims, my brother's adult children's lives would be forever changed, forever scarred, forever minimized because of gun violence. It's devastating.....I pray for the victims and their families. I pray for all who are broken to be healed. I pray for common sense gun control. I pray for peace. SHALOM.

ABOUT THE CREASEY MAHAN NATURE PRESERVE

Creasey Mahan Nature Preserve is located at 12501 Harmony Landing Road located in beautiful Goshen, Kentucky, which is approximately 30 minutes east of Louisville, Kentucky and 20 minutes west of La Grange, Kentucky. Creasey Mahan Nature Preserve is a non-profit public charity established in 1975 through the legacy of Virginia Creasey Mahan and Howard Mahan. The Nature Preserve is a 170-acre family friendly destination in Goshen that offers a complete family experience. In 2017 alone, 48,000 visitors were served through monthly events, school field trips, athletic practices and races, fun programs, and community gatherings.

The Preserve maintains three historic buildings and offers a natural history museum for educational programs. With over 9 miles of wooded trails that weave through open grasslands and four year-round springs and waterfalls, Creasey Mahan Nature Preserve is a wonderful place to relax and take a leisurely hike. Families may enjoy using Harmony Park playground, and visit the library in the Preserve's old dairy and tobacco barn. They may also have a picnic, camp overnight, walk their dog(s), and fly a kite in one of the open grassy areas. Creasey Mahan Nature Preserve offers something for everyone!

For more information, please visit:
http://www.creaseymahannaturepreserve.org

Creasey Mahan Nature Preserve
12501 Harmony Landing Road
Goshen, Kentucky 40026
Phone: 502-228-4362
General email: Info@KYNaturepreserve.org

CREASEY MAHAN NATURE PRESERVE MAP

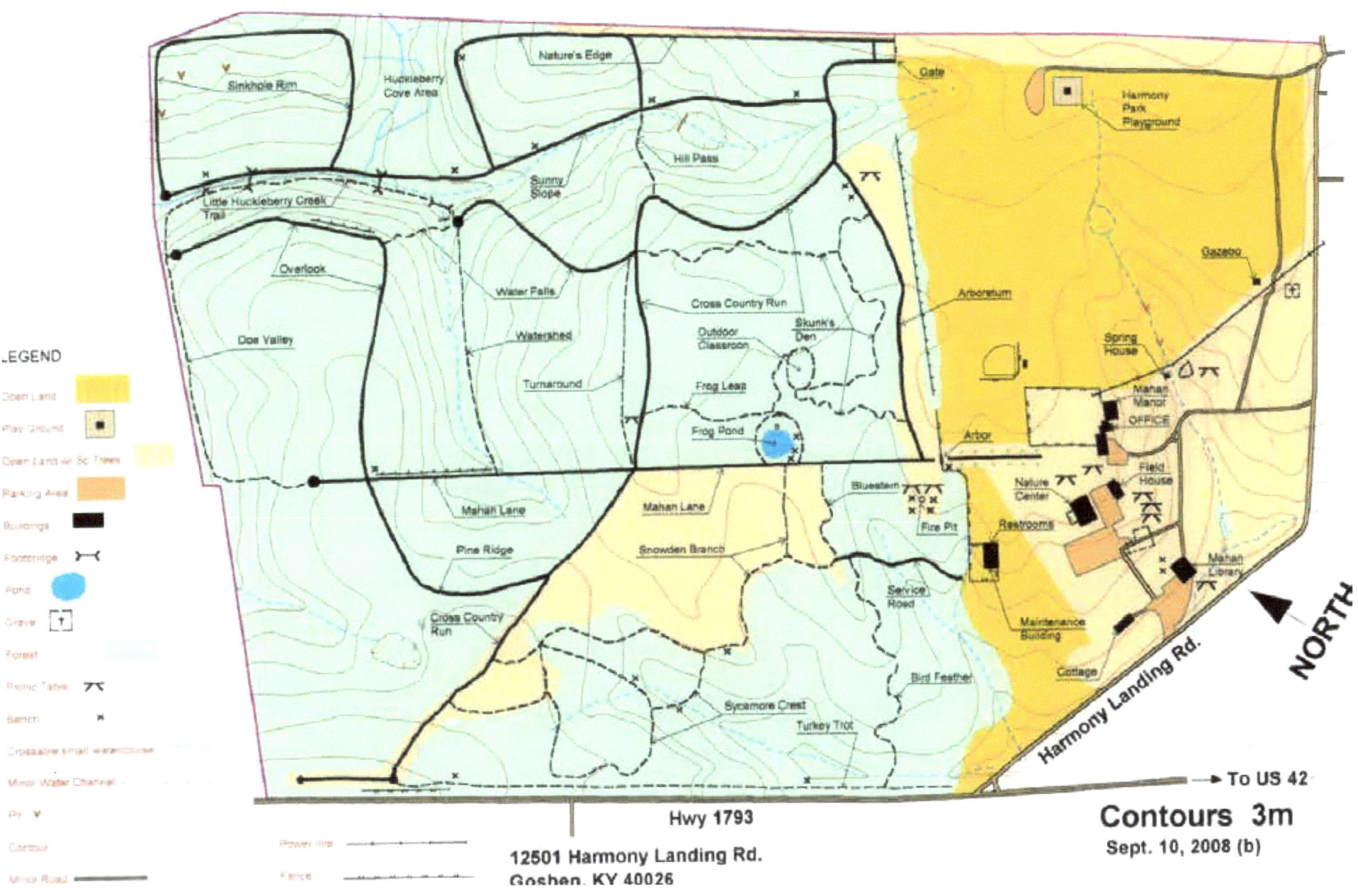

www.ingramcontent.com/pod-product-compliance
Lightning Source LLC
Chambersburg PA
CBHW041644220426

43661CB00018B/1292